For Jim. —
You've been there
since the beginning for me
Thank you!

Loneliness Among Primates

Loneliness Among Primates

by

Alexander Payne Morgan

Kelsay Books

Cover design: Shay Culligan

Cover Photograph: "Trees Under Water"
by Alexander Payne Morgan

ISBN: 978-1-949229-11-0

Kelsay Books
Aldrich Press
www.kelsaybooks.com

To
Maria Costantini, Margo LaGattuta,
and Nancy Williams
in blessed memory

Acknowledgments

Grateful acknowledgment is made to the editors of the following journals where these poems first appeared:

Bayou Magazine: "The Slave Owner's Daughter Makes Soap"
The Dead Mule School of Southern Literature: "A Sandspur," "Sorry, I've Got to Go"
Dunes Review: "Programmers for the End of the World," "Last Lunch" (as the ending of the story "Tablecloth")
The MacGuffin: "The Mathematician's Daughter," "Ulysses: The Thinker"
Peninsular Poets: "Postponed Divorce"
Peacock Review: "The Costumer's Husband: Tech Week"
Sequestrum: "Dungeons and Dragons"

"Ulysses: The Thinker" was an Honorable Mention in the 2013 National Poet Hunt contest judged by Philip Levine.
"The Cup" won first prize in the Springfed Arts writing contest (poetry) 2015.
"The Mathematician's Daughter" was the Detroit Working Writers MacGuffin Poetry Prize Winner 2016.
"Postponed Divorce" took third place in the category *Love* of the *Peninsula Poets* 2016 contest.
"The Slave Owner's Daughter Makes Soap" was awarded the 2016 Kay Murphy Prize for Poetry by *Bayou Magazine.*

Mary Jo Firth Gillett's workshops have been an invaluable starting point for many of these poems. Thank you, Mary Jo, for your encouragement and suggestions over the years. Thank you also to workshop leaders Mary Ann Wehler and Lucinda Sabino and to the participants in all my poetry workshops. You have been so kind and so helpful.

Ken Meisel enormously enhanced my parental prestige by praising my work to my daughter's high school English class. Thank you for that, Ken, and for all your other support and encouragement.

I want to acknowledge everybody who contributes to the amazing Detroit literary community. Thank you, John D. Lamb and M.L. Liebler, for making Springfed Arts and the Detroit Writers' Guild such important parts of that community.

Thanks also to my fellow writers, including David Strong, Diane DeCillis, Bethany Schryburt, Terry Blackhawk, and Nancy Owen Nelson for support, encouragement, and helpful criticism.

Special thanks—I can't say enough—to Joy Gaines-Friedler, my teacher, mentor, and friend.

The Vermont College of Fine Arts Postgraduate Writers' Conference (summer, 2017) helped shape this volume to its final form. Thank you, Matthew Dickman and my workshop participants.

Charlotte Pence's suggestions in her Black Lawrence Press consultation were especially helpful. Thank you, Charlotte.

I'm proud to have shared so much of my life with Janice, Abraham, and Julia. I love you. And thank you, dear Janice, for always being there to keep me going and for sharing the occasional pint of Ben and Jerry's after a long day of writing.

Contents

The Cup

A little brown ceramic thing she'd turned,
added a handle
mailed to me for my birthday
maybe to make a point about her independence,
her maiden name sharp on the bottom, and maybe
to reconnect with me
her ex.

I didn't thank her or otherwise acknowledge the gift.
I wanted her, not
cryptic negotiations fired in clay like cuneiform.

Then I heard that she was sick,
and soon she was herself
no more than clay.

One day, for no reason
I began to use her cup.
I liked the way its small dry circumference
fit my palm in the morning
though
to use it cast a risk.

I couldn't help imagining
exiting my car
hands full and fumbling
sudden and unexpected shards
broadcast across the concrete driveway
scattered beyond reassembly.

But it didn't happen that way. I had my hands full
that part was right
mind adrift laid all down on the kitchen table: the grocery bag,

the book, the other book, the file folder, the keys, the cup
dropped, maybe from the height of only one inch, onto its side, and
a large wedge-shaped piece popped out

perhaps along fault lines
present from the beginning.

I glued it back. It
drips. It doesn't matter.

What Good Are Pigeons?

We're going on a trip
me
my older brother, Avery
and Mommy.
I bring Urnk
my stuffed elephant.

We ride on a train!
Step down under an arching roof
to a giant room
millions of people
and pigeons.

Urnk wants to chase the pigeons
so we do.

I see Daddy.
He lives in New York City.
We live in Pennsylvania.
There's going to be a divorce.

Daddy waves.
Comes forward.
His long brown coat with the big buttons.
His fedora.
His smile.

Mommy stands
looking down, looking up, her face
sad and squinting.

Daddy lifts his arms
as if to offer her a hug
then lets it go.

Did you have to bring them?
Okay. Okay.
The appointment's at noon.
I've got a cab waiting.
Posh doctor, he
does this all the time
for Tammany girlfriends
and careless sopranos.
No trouble. No complications.
Not even that much dough.

Mommy isn't listening.
I want to keep this child.

We all stop.
Even the pigeons
seem to freeze.

Daddy gets terrified eyes.
Be reasonable.

His fallen smile comes back
a tough kid's grin.
You can't do this.
We're going to split.
Your fault.
Crazy.

His voice scratches
like nails on concrete,
shuffles like flapping wings,
loses itself like cooing in a crowd.

Mommy turns,
pulls us away.

The baby grew up
an odd bird, a dumb cluck,
unable to scratch his own feed or scout his own coop,
a predator's easy meal.

Dad corners Avery and me.
You know I was right.
I'm just saying
I was right. I was right. I was right.

The Slave Owner's Daughter Makes Soap

Savannah, 1950

Slaves were worth more than railroad investment, banks and factories nationwide combined in 1860.
Corey Brooks, York College Professor of History

I see with five-year-old eyes:
    a wood fire under a cauldron,
    a red round box of lye powder,
    old tin cans filled with bacon fat.

Granny's daddy's slaves used to do this work,
but they got freed
before my granny got born,
she the seventh white daughter
of a white gentleman, bitter
how he got robbed of his property.

Granny jabs her broomstick with two hands.
Her loose hair sprays as she
works the mash,
grips the sandy dirt bare-toed,
strains out her neck,
forces the soap hard. Then
she cuts the remnant
scum into bite-sized squares.

I say:
    Are those squares candy?

Mommy explodes like blood from a whipping:
    Don't touch that stuff.
    It'll rot your fingers off,
    eat your tongue gone,
    burn your eyes
    to black pools of pus.

Granny chuckles:

Little boy,
other side Savannah,
ate some lye soap once.
Burned his throat right out,
had to go round with blue strings
tied out his nose.

Granny loves her terrible stories:

a gasoline cigar lighter exploded, burned her uncle
burned his face right off;
lady next door dusting her new electric lamp,
unplugged, but it electrocuted her anyway;
little paperboy crashed his bicycle, his head
wedged in a culvert,
died when they tried to pry him free.

Her stories stick like scum
in my brain for decades,
for decades until I can realize
the bitter glee of her father,
her father's ferocious disbelief as his world inverted.

Mommy sulks,
while Granny stores the soap in her wood crate,
a rough pine box,
the kind oranges come in.

She picks up and puts down
the nasty little soap squares bare-handed.
Lost in the rhythm of long practice,
she doesn't give a spit how much they burn.

Big Sister

For nine months you knew our mother's voice.
She sang to you and gave you the comfort of her beating heart.

You took air only a few moments, lungs sputtering.

Did you have time to spit rage? Curse your inept maker?
Did you love? I hope so.
                                        In my heart's movie, you hold
my hand to cross streets, praise my crayoned dinosaur,
teach me to play Candyland and Monopoly,
boss me around, but I like it.

Some nights, when I'm out watching the stars,
I merge sideways, elsewhere,
and sense you simply stepped away, that soon
we'll be arguing again about Mother
and high school and whatever else passes
for important.

Last Lunch

Savannah, 1953

Daddy came sometimes at Christmas time, and once
when I was eight he took me out to lunch.

We enter the cathedral space
of the Desoto Hotel dining room.
A long black coat and bow tie jump up, animated
by my daddy's silver dollar.

Two button eyes on the back of the coat
lead us to our table.

Tablecloth
starched white cotton.
Thick. Ironed. Like a heavy bed sheet.
Enormous napkins
folded into stiff fans.

Plates
delicate. Pale as polished shell.
Big and little spoons.
Big and little and tiny forks.

Daddy threw his plate
against the wall…
Mother'd scraped the carrots
wrong.

"May I recommend the crab cakes, sir? Coffee?"
"A Manhattan."

Daddy catches my eye,
sweeps his hand to all the room.
"This do?"

I touch the cloth
run my hand over it,
feel the thickness of its threads.
Nothing in our house shines
so white and clean.
I whisper,
"Wonderful, Daddy."

Mother in bed with her books,
door closed.
Breakfast milk stiffens
as the heat rises.

At nearby tables, men in strange pale suits talk of dog racing
and Florida. Women laugh, squirm
in layered dresses, stretch to show
pink-painted toe nails in high-heeled sandals.

Daddy smiling tells me
how he once was boss of all the boys,

how he built a boat, beat
the tides and waves, the twists and turns
of the Intracoastal Waterway,

how he defied the stinging salt and sun
to dredge for rare anemones
with an apparatus of his own invention,

how he learned the trick to save
those slight specimens for a shelf he'd built
himself in his backyard laboratory,

when he was a boy, like me, in Savannah.

The tablecloth I will discover
has a tablecloth underneath.

Idiot Waters

My little brother visits the school psychiatrist.

Words are slippery fish, dart
for wider seas.

Idiot once meant selfish,
too stupid to comprehend the communal good.

Then, it swam into doctors' waters
where my brother, Jamesie
was netted
put in that pool
for his own good.

The term has not always been applied to him
with clinical sympathy.
His face holds the perpetual
hurt smile of the bullied
retard.

If that word *retard* bothers you,
I don't mind if you find another.
Call him "cognitively challenged" or whatever
pleases.

But really, I think
you should go ahead
and call him an idiot,
to comprehend, to appreciate
his daily passage.

No language monkey play
will sun-brighten his hidden places,
fend off the children
who grin to make him bleed.

Ulysses: The Thinker

Valdosta, Georgia, 1960

Ulee is just the black janitor
who's swept the halls of Valdosta High School
since before forever
takes his time, observes his white work
situation with slow eyes, allows
the days to pass, likes his indoor job
where the Klan
the Cyclops, the sheriff
won't grin and question.

The yearbook photographer, Robert
poses Ulee as Rodin's "The Thinker" sitting
hand on chin, elbow on knee. Robert
giggling.

Ulee poses, doesn't object, holding still
maintains a tense forbearance, thinks
about the little rented house he
his wife and children might be turned out of
if he objects, thinks
how he gives his wife money
for food and doesn't tell her anything, thinks
of how his children run to greet him
when he gets off the bus
and hug him and call him "sir," because
he's taught them something of respect, thinks
when he's cleaning up after the white people's children
he can't afford to object to anything.

Yet, he thinks
too, of one day when he might choose
to string his bow.

A Sandspur

magnified is a rod of spikes.
I know. I took the photomicrograph they used
in the Valdosta High School yearbook for years after I fled.
An eccentric icon for a high school,
you might say, but a certain rough humor
was de rigueur in that territory.

Backlighted, it's strangely translucent. The stem
leads upward on a slant. The barbs appear
too rounded at this magnification to penetrate,
but they'll stick fine at their own scale,
as you try to clear your socks
or your brain,
whichever the most compelling penetration.

There was Coach J who liked ripe reddened
boy asses. I hated his grin. He got run
out of town sometime around 1961.
And the thirty-year-tenured Bible-quoting
Miss R who gave girls A's, boys D's,
finally fired, finally, the year before the year
she would have spiked me on her D.

Sandspur sap flows with why complain
when you'll be the one gets the blame.

But like I say, you had to take hold of the humor
as you ended each day picking out the sharp
spine-covered burrs.

To a Father Thirteen Years Dead

Athens, Greece, 1992

I fly a great distance to talk with your best friend,
your second wife nice enough
to provide his name and number.

Bushy white eyebrows, face creased with humor
and sun, he meets me
with pleased astonishment: *pleased* because he

loved you, *astonished* because he has never heard of me.

I walk next day to the ancient Athenian cemetery
with its weeping statues, its lichen-mottled Greek crosses,
its stunted cypresses, its feral dogs fighting

over something still struggling.

And me
walking off
the aftershocks.

I hadn't even been *alive* enough to you
for you to tell your friend I was alive,
he, who'd known you since you'd played stickball together

barefoot on dirt Savannah streets
before his family gave up on America.

But you, trans-Atlantic affluent,
he'd met and teased all the children
of your second family.

I like your friend.
I feel the years of his loss
like a street kid
discovering the benefit of shoes.

My Rashomon

after Kurosawa's 1950 film, Rashomon.

The film shows various characters providing subjective, alternative, self-serving and contradictory versions of the same incident.

I recognize the cocky bandit as my father.
His bold charm
takes what it wants, blows a kiss,
slips away.

My mother, the wife,
stands on her virtue.
Her story must be swallowed,
or she savages us with her indignation.

The samurai's ghost, my father's afterimage,
his smiles, his hugs,
his presents.
I, dumb as a horse, wait for him to remember.

My big brother, the woodcutter,
a petty thief himself but
claims the baby. He
grins at my confusion.

Little brother also robs us.
His idiot outbursts make us outcasts.
Mother obsesses for his cure.
Our pitiful resources exhausted.

I play the priest,
horrified by the rape and murder
or, as some might claim, the fight and seduction.

The rain stops, the sun shines,
our dissonant stories mockingly unresolved.

The End.

Sorry, I've Got to Go

Malo Mori Quam Foedari (I choose death over dishonor)
Payne Family Motto

The sun hits the wall of the little nest
my new wife has made of our flat
on Bishop Street, and the light angles
across the old pine floor. March wind
flexes the plastic tacked to the windows,
but Heather, wise in the ways of cats,
has curled up in a plank of sun, and sleeps.

I'm holding the just-arrived with no stamp
single-page onionskin government letter.
Despite jokes and rumors, it doesn't say "Greetings."
I'm frozen.

Carol King looks across barefoot from her record cover.
Dylan's head explodes with psychedelic delirium,
a poster we've thumbtacked over our mattress.

Heather yawns and stretches.

We've argued all year about Canada
or prison, the hard moral choices,
or that psychiatrist in Boston who'll write
insane diagnoses, or other
convoluted options.
All that hot talk now stilled
by this one cold paper blade.

Somewhere in me, old blood
pumps with martial obligation.
It’s so stupid—it’s not even the right war—but no
choice. Never had one. This translucent typed order
nullifies evasion.

I know I’ll let them take me.

Programmers for the End of the World

after "Dreamers" by Siegfried Sassoon

There are still some 26,000 nuclear warheads in the world, enough to destroy civilization many times over and destroy most life on earth.
Nuclear Age Peace Foundation, 2013

Ballistic soldiers live for one day's ash.
Their algebra can tune the toxic flames
encoded in each hardened silo's lash.
They chill with comics, pizza, beer, and games;
next day, their skill maps out countdown conditions.
Shadows over glowing tubes, they calculate
to maximize the fallout cloud dispersions.

The day comes:

TVs cars kids friends wives evaporate.

And after:

In rubble remnants fit for dying rats,
their misused genius all unhinged by pain,
they'll cry for Facebook friends and smart-phone chats,
be damned they couldn't harden to retain:
soft fluttering curtains, washed dishes, lazy cats,
holidays, Hollywood, Hersey bars, and clean rain.

Coming Home

after Stephen Dunn

Most days
my family's dug in with
TV and headsets and homework. The goldfish
is busy patrolling his perimeter.
I move like him:
shuffle papers, probe the Internet,
scrounge for leftovers. But tonight

we all who are not fish
crawl out of our bunkers.
Love, a prisoner of circumstance,
has been set free.

My wife's smile offers me an unexpected grace.
My hands reach for her flanks, and suddenly
we cling as if I'd come again from war, the sand
still settling off my uniform.
Abe and Julia break us up
shouting "Shabbat Shalom" and "Group Hug"
jostling and giggling.

Weary of the week
our separate skirmishes suspended,
we face each other across the dinner table,
grinning despite what's past,
for no reason laughing.

“Death Stinks”

eight-year-old Julia comes to tell me,
a complaint more properly addressed to God.

In His absence I listen, struck,
having nothing to add
but vague concurrence.

Later, I see her drawings
of people at the point of dying,
their souls hovering ghosts
with angels above as if to harvest.

The corpses’ eyes are X’s,
since they no longer see,
the ghosts’ sockets forlorn O’s.

The angels gather, efficient but aloof,
minding their own business.

Where to Be Blue

Julia, now fifteen, has blue hair.

I agreed. The master hair man bleached, blued,
blew, billed $200. Gladly, I
paid his price. If you've got to be blue,
let it be your hair.

When I was fifteen, they called me bitter.

I was

supposed to know what the elders believed
and act like I believed it, too. Something
in me rebelled from lying. Disobedience
led to whipping. I could accept my pain
but not their glee.

The pedophilic coaches, the tight lipped marms,
they preached tough love, but love or rape,
it felt the same to me.
Mute as an inmate
tunneling, I in spoonfuls dug my long escape.

My daughter doesn't have to care
if I like her new blue hair.
What she wants to do, what she
needs to do, is wave her defiant
locks: blue, breezy, styled like
an un-tortured child.

The Mathematician's Daughter

Only in the hurricane of her next day's test
will she let me talk prime numbers,
logarithms, triangles and surds.
She detests my lovely mathematics,

my play, my toil.
Yet I can't help but hope she'll be beguiled.

Look: x-2 splits this polynomial
to birth a factor child... But no.
She wants no lyric explanations.

Just tell me what I need to pass the test.

Like a werewolf at full moon, I change
from a lover of pure form
into that flat-footed monster of pedagogy,
the bloody rote-memorization coach.

When you see this, do that.
When you see that, do this.

Empty clumps of symbols
float in some salt mental sea
until spewed on the blank beach of a test,
abandoned, forgotten, left to rot.

I still sneak in some sweet tangent sections,
unmask a few unexpected variations,
ta-dah! a pair of cute osculations.

Soon, she's had enough of me and math,
but I can't stop, can't get it out of my head.
See how this primal puzzle comes apart?
See how quadratic curves can map to rings?

She loved the end
of *The Lion, the Witch, and the Wardrobe*,
us snuggled together on the bed, her delight
as time snapped back to childhood,
her smile at the paradox surprise.

Caught in the arc of my own persistent heart,
I long to find a formula unfolding
to give her that same joy.

Loneliness Among Primates

A male uses such aggression to train a female to fear him so that she will be more likely to surrender to his subsequent sexual advances.
"Apes of Wrath" by Barbara Smuts, Discover Magazine, *August 1995*

The male attacks, full snarling, spraying spit
enraged, engorged, huge to the young female,
drags kicks then throws her down, leans face to face.
She cries and cringes as he mimes a bite.

He rejoins the guys, picking up their game.
She's folded fetal, a kicked child quivering
in the clay her whistling breath like soft crying
watches cowering. When will he come again?

The primatologist folds up her pad,
picks up her pack and gun, hikes back to base.
A colleague snickers as he lets her pass.
She hands the chem-tech guy her bag of scat.

Inside her tent, she types her notes, devours
her lunch, and marks an X for one less day.

My Son Doesn't Do His Homework

My son
takes the school bus home
his skin sweating acid.
I wait to offer the smile he'll sometimes return, the hug
he'll sometimes allow.

After supper
my damned duty's to
remind him
his school day's
not yet done.

My son who
gags on the rubrics
of the obedience prison
resists coughing up the bribe.
He loses himself in fantasy games
like a surrounded soldier playing solitaire,
oblivious to the coming dawn.

I am terrified he will find no safe passage,
no tunnel, no airlift, no band of brothers,
and I know the enemy will crush any soul
caught under its tread.

He's chosen a strategy
I can't follow.
I can't follow
what he's going to.

My son's bus
I see coming down Pierce Street.
The next stop is his.
I shape my mouth to make
some kind of smile.

Dungeons and Dragons

My brother Avery greets me beaming, offering me his phone.
A sultry-voiced voice mail, *Baby, I miss you already…*
He's beaming, but I fear a basilisk arising.
Five wives, four divorces, but this time (I thought) safe at home.

A sultry-voiced chimera, *Baby, I miss you already…*
My son loves to roll the dice for *Dungeons and Dragons* with his uncle.
Five wives, four divorces, but this time (I hoped) safe at home.
I know my brother. Another adventure. Soon, no place to see my son.

My son loves to join dwarves, dryads, and djinns with his uncle.
In a quirky play of genes, my son's a gambler like my brother.
I know my brother. Another bad marriage. No place to see my son.
I'd been hoping he could mentor the boy I cannot reach.

In a quirky play of genes, my son's a gamester like my brother.
She's got this tight little body, my brother brags, he taunts.
I'd been hoping he could mentor the boy I cannot reach.
Avery grins. *What can I do? I love women.* His grin to me a skull.

She's got this tight little body, he brags, he taunts.
His wife—the boring homemaker—made a home for a board of magical creatures.
He's grinning. *What can I do? I love women.* He won't admit the skull.
My son asks his uncle how to manage harpies and medusas.

Avery's angry wife—I've seen this all before—will bar her home to magical creatures.
My son loves to talk tactics for zombies and trolls with his uncle.
He asks his uncle—he wouldn't ask me—about harpies and medusas.
Girlfriend's apartment a bed for a different board of gaming.

My son loves to talk tactics for zombies and trolls with his uncle.
Avery pushes the photo in my face. *Congratulate me.* A picture of gamine vitality.
Girlfriend's apartment a realm for a different run of gaming.
How could I admire this picture of the charm he'll cast to ruins?

Congratulate me, my brother commands. I see she's like my son, a packet of playful vitality.
I never know what Avery wants from me. *I see what you mean,* I say and turn away.
He smiles at praise, doesn't catch how I feel about the charm he'll cast to ruins.
It *means* something, Thursday nights with his uncle for *Dungeons and Dragons*.

I want Avery to care, but my son for him is just a token on his way.
Avery's beaming, doesn't sense the basilisk arising.
It *meant* something, Thursday nights with his uncle for *Dungeons and Dragons*.
My brother Avery still beaming, still offering me his phone.

Postponed Divorce

after "Metaphor" by Claudia Emerson

We didn't think what drew us—just
        hearts churning, softer than grievance.

The clock you threw made a scattered draw,
        the parts on the floor a guilty

incompleteness that now you could not
        leave. You came in, gave me one look,

and pulled off your dress, crying,
        then folded yourself into my arms. I wanted

you to come back—until you did.

Daughter Terminated

In a crowd I see you.
You don’t see me,
then you pass out of sight.

You would be
around forty now,
although you look younger.

Such parents:
a father haunted by his father,
by equations;
a mother by incest, by rages,
dead at thirty-five.

Of course, had you been,
you would have been a factor.

Even a fluttering of initial conditions
can nudge the course of vortices.

Your beating heart could have tipped
our course away from strife,
her course away from cancer.

Maybe you’ll recognize me the next time we pass,
give me your mother’s wonderful smile.

The Costumer's Husband: Tech Week

after "The Shipfitter's Wife" by Dorianne Laux

I love her most
when she comes home past midnight,
eye lashes trailing glitter,
fingers sticky with the residue of two-sided tape,
her smock, one of my discarded shirts, rainbowed
around the pocket, smelling of marker,
paints and glues, the fresh cut cloth
of final alterations.
                                        I go to her where she slumps
on the red ladder-chair in the kitchen, her fists
cracked-turquoise nail polish clinging to car keys
and release those fingers and offer chamomile tea,
a slice of orange, a bit of lightly buttered challah toast.

Then I lead her to bed and
free her of all remaining encumbrances,
take in my arms the flailing panic
of missing props and missed cues, improvised
wigs and fast-shaped hats, half-hung drapes
in the shouted improvisation of lights on ladders,
the quick-change fittings, the re-fittings,
the hot mercy of the glue gun, the genius of Velcro,
the director's tense uncomplimentary dismissal,
and the long drive home.

Missed Funerals

1941
Sunk by a sub off Savannah,
Daddy's little brother, Uncle Alex,
wartime merchantman's second engineer, oceanographer
if he hadn't been blown up and drowned.
They had a memorial service for him
even though he wasn't there.
Me neither,
but I got his name.

1950
Laid out, *Papou* was creepy,
my big brother said,
he old enough for my father's father's funeral.
Not me or my two cousins.
We watched ants plow sand in the cracks of the bricks of the
    sidewalk in front of *Yiayia*'s house.

1965
As kids we had squirmed in sweet-but-boring *Yiayia*'s meticulous
    parlor, while the grownups talked,
and no toys.
By the time she died my parents were divorced.
Mother didn't want to face our dad
except in anger.
We stayed away.

1971
In the army I held my breath
underwater, under pressure, under military law.
Mother's long distance call a long wet wire.
Her father gone. What could that mean underwater?
I asked if she wanted me there.
She said it was up to me.

1978
My mother's mother gave her snort.
"How long you gonna wanna play with that thing?"
Her tone turned my lovely little HO train to shit,
her grin full of jack-o'-lantern malice.
Mother didn't ask me to honor her remains.
I didn't ask if she wanted me to.

1979
Dad died all at once on the beach,
his second wife said.
She had opened my last little letter of filiation,
sent before I knew that he had died.
Ten years later,
his daughter told me they had loosed his ashes
in the ocean where he liked to fish.

1984
My mother's older brother knocked her down and raped her,
ripped off second-grade Linda's panties, offered fifth-grade Mathew a dollar for a suck.
I don't remember what he offered me.
Mother forgave her poor brother in the name of Jesus,
didn't stop him,
didn't bother tell me when he'd passed to his reward.

1985
I was the only man she knew.
We divorced
and then she died.

Her mother hated me,
would have hated any thief.
I loved her smile.
She's buried.
I don’t know where.

Music for the Fading Light

> *That mortal is a fool who, prospering, thinks his life has any strong foundation.*
>
> *Euripides,* The Trojan Women

Once, the summer daylight went so slow, while
she and I in wisteria shade blessed our grapes and our children,
laughed and walked as we watched the slant sun skim old brick,
bring out its reassuring glow,
and the ironwork's intricate shadows painted curious traces,

and even as the sky would shift from cyan to cerulean to cobalt,
she and I would mark Jupiter rising, sharp over the trees, old god,
    proud,
and we could still make our way home swatting at the twilight
    awareness—
pretending we were merely bothered by mosquitoes—
that people don't always find what they expect to come home to.

We won't pray, but we could seek refuge in the mystery of a
    temple.
She and I understand sacrifice, might even hold the knife
to the throat of an unblemished bull
to bribe an oasis of days,
days we won't otherwise be allocated.

We shared Summer-of-Love delusions, but that's all past, except
she and I recently discovered broadcasting between Venus
and Earth from a deserted robot satellite station
the old songs on an infinite loop,
the old canticles of hopeful defiance.

Time, that raptor, a god's eagle, soars, rips, weaves history.
She and I remember how like surprised Jews burned out
and scattered by fanatics
we lost the comfort of pretending

we could protect ourselves by praying.

All we ask now is to share a bit more sweetness.
She and I won't praise, but we will beg to be allowed
a blessing of last-minute shade and laughter.
Sometimes, even the grudging primal gods granted
mortal fools one last skim of summer sun before the sacking.

The Meaning of Leaves

Beside the upright stones,
their carved Hebrew blurred, unreadable
even in the slant November sun,
the little boy
finds a pile of leaves
and begins
a careful un-raking.

He’s pleased with his leaves
purposeful
puzzling out
his ordering on the sidewalk of
flat red maple fingers
curled brown elm tears
pliant yellow gingko fans.

The final prayer doesn't jar his focus nor does
the sun-touched falling of more red, brown, and gold
whose luminosity is its own blessing.
He works
unaware
even as shoveled dirt drums on a pinewood lid.

He's too surprised
to cry
when his Daddy scoops him up
to go.

About the Author

Alexander Payne Morgan was born in Savannah, Georgia. His poems have been published in *The MacGuffin*, *Crack The Spine*, *Dunes Review,* and *The Dead Mule School of Southern Literature,* among others. He was awarded the 2016 Kay Murphy Prize for Poetry by *Bayou Magazine* and the 2016 Detroit Working Writers *MacGuffin* Poetry Prize. He's a member of Detroit Working Writers, Detroit Writers' Guild, Michigan Writers, the Poetry Society of Michigan, and Springfed Arts. He is a retired industrial mathematician.